RAILWAY HISTORY IN PICTURES: NORTH-EAST ENGLAND

The south end of York station in the summer of 1904, with trains headed by North Eastern, Midland, Great Eastern, and Great Northern locomotives. The signalbox is the old Locomotive Yard box, closed on 13 June 1909 and replaced by a new box with the same name a short distance further south; this in turn lasted until 1951. The platforms are at their intermediate length; later they were extended as far as the signalbox in this view. In producing the painting from a known photograph the artist has altered the aspect of the signals at the end of Platform 4.

RAILWAY HISTORY IN PICTURES

North-East England

K. HOOLE

DAVID & CHARLES : NEWTON ABBOT

7153 4317 3

Printed in Great Britain by
E. Goodman & Son Limited Taunton
for David & Charles (Publishers) Limited
South Devon House Newton Abbot Devon

CONTENTS

INTRODUCTION

The north east has two faces—the grimy, smoky appearance it presents on Tees-side and Tyneside, and the beauty of the dales, moors and coastline. Fortunately it does not take long to get from the industrial area into the countryside, but sometimes it is impossible not to see signs of industry in the distance. However, even the smoking chimneys of Consett have a certain beauty when viewed from miles away at the now almost derelict railway township of Waskerley, way up on the wild moors.

And yet in some parts of the north east it is possible to be far away from industry and now, unfortunately, from a railway. Most of the country branches have disappeared . . . often replaced by the red *United* bus . . . but the north east has been well covered by photographers over the last century and more. This volume, therefore, is an attempt to present a composite picture of the railways, large and small, as they were. It complements my *Regional History of the Railways of Great Britain Volume 4 - The North East*, in which the full story was described in words and maps, but with many further illustrations.

Most of these photographs are from my own files built up during forty years' interest in the railways of the north east counties.

THE BEAUTIFUL NORTH EAST

Much of the north east is disfigured by industry but very much more is unspoilt beautiful countryside. Unfortunately, one of the most picturesque lines, that between Pickering and Grosmont, is now closed. Between Pickering and Levisham one track was removed in 1917 for use in France but never replaced. Here is a Whitby to York train about to enter on the single line at Levisham.

Another picturesque route was the former Whitby, Redcar & Middlesbrough Union line between Whitby and Loftus. This ran along the coast and at Sandsend the station was on the edge of the cliffs. The line was closed in 1958 and the interesting iron viaducts were demolished. The picture shows a Scarborough-bound train standing in Sandsend station. Sandsend Ness is in the background, with traces of old alum workings.

THE INDUSTRIAL NORTH EAST

Much of the north east's industry has developed from coal and shipping, although coal mining is now a declining industry. The major rivers of the north east .   .   .   the Humber, Tees, Wear and Tyne—have all played their part in this development but have also proved to be barriers as far as land transport has been concerned. Here we see a combination of river, road and rail at Lambton Staiths, on the south bank of the Wear at Sunderland. These staiths closed in 1967.

The photograph was taken from the footplate of a National Coal Board engine, with the NER railway bridge of 1879 in the foreground and the road bridge (renewed in 1929) further downstream.

For use between collieries and the coal staiths in Northumberland the NER introduced double-bogie hopper wagons with a 40 ton capacity. A number of these were fitted with automatic brakes and trial runs with both Westinghouse and vacuum fitted trains were made between York and Scarborough in October 1903. Here is vacuum fitted Class T 162 at Bootham Junction, with the train standing on the Hull line.

(Left) Fifty Class T1 engines were sent to France in World War I and on their return were fitted with the insignia of the Royal Engineers, together with three service stripes.

(Below) The largest NER 0-8-0s were the Class T3 engines designed by Raven. Here is 901 on a mineral train at Cowton in 1921.

In a number of cases the NER was prepared to allow colliery owners to work their own traffic to the docks over NER metals. This arrangement continued under LNER ownership, and finally under British Railways and the National Coal Board. The most extensive use of this co-operation was by the Lambton network around Sunderland and here NCB 10 passes through Pallion station on its way from Penshaw to Sunderland.

(Below) Although not a native of the north east mention must be made of the BR 9F 2-10-0 stationed at Tyne Dock shed from 1956, which put in some excellent work on the iron ore trains to Consett. These trains of 9 wagons, each with a tare weight of 29 tons and a loaded weight of up to 85 tons, had to be worked up gradients as steep as 1 in 35. To accomplish this a 2-10-0 was required at front and rear of each train. The illustration shows 92060 and 92065 near Stanley in 1956.

PASSENGER TRAFFIC

The NER had an extensive passenger service, ranging from the heavy east coast expresses on the main line to the remote country branches. There were also many important cross-country branches and here is an unidentified 2-2-2 at Heslerton, between Scarborough and York. The photograph was taken about 1871 . . . deduced from the fact that this was the time at which an upper floor was added to the station house. Note the low platform: these still remain at some stations on the branch, although a higher platform was later provided as an extension. Passenger services were withdrawn from Heslerton in 1930.

No 190 started life in 1849 but was extensively rebuilt in 1881, although remaining as a single: it is illustrated in this 1881 form. The engine was again rebuilt in 1894 and appeared as a 2-2-4T for use on official inspection saloon duties: in this form it ran until 1936. Note the direction signal on the extreme right.

NER locomotives were long-lived, although often this was on paper only. Many new locomotives were classed as rebuilds for accountancy purposes, taking the number of an earlier engine and assuming its history. However, 252, originally built by Robert Stephenson & Co in 1840 as a 2-2-2 tender engine, could have been a rebuild rather than a renewal into the 2-2-2T form illustrated. It is seen attached to an inspection saloon c 1870 and was withdrawn in 1894 after being successively renumbered 1931 and 1735.

(Below) No 319 was the famous *Jenny Lind* of the York & North Midland Railway, built by E. B. Wilson & Co of Leeds in 1847. The photograph is reputed to have been taken at Scarborough in 1876 when the engine was working the first NER stores train. By this time the engine had lost its name but still retained the handsome fluted dome cover used by Wilson.

From 1874, many NER branches were worked by the successful Fletcher 0-4-4WT, later known as Class BTP. Altogether 124 were built, both by the NER and by contractors. Many of them were later fitted with push-and-pull gear for working steam autocars and 188 is seen on such a working at Beck Hole in 1908. This single-platform station was situated on the original course of the Whitby & Pickering Railway, at the foot of the Goathland incline. The incline was replaced by a locomotive worked line in 1869 but in 1908 a summer-only passenger service was introduced between Whitby and Beck Hole, using autocars . . . the NER title for a push-and-pull worked train.

The best photographer of NER trains pre-1914 was undoubtedly the late R. J. Purves. He spent a lifetime in the signalling department of the NER and its successors and took most of his fine action shots around Newcastle, particularly at the Gateshead end of the King Edward Bridge. However, this shot was taken south of York and shows a Scarborough-Leeds express near Chaloner Whin junction.

Another fine photograph by R. J. Purves shows Class R1 4-4-0 1244 passing Low Fell on an up express.

An unusual task for a single-driver was the use of 2-2-4T 957 on a York-Hull express of two coaches in 1934. This was originally a Class BTP 0-4-4WT (see 188 at Beck Hole, opposite) but it was rebuilt in 1903 for use on inspection specials. Until scrapped in 1937 it was stationed at Hull Botanic Gardens shed and occasionally used as a replacement for the Armstrong-Whitworth diesel-electric railcar *Lady Hamilton*.

The North Eastern introduced atlantics in 1903 and they worked all the most important trains over the ensuing twenty years. There were four varieties: 1792 was to the original Class V design by Wilson Worsdell. It is seen at the head of a Royal train, heading south on the Stephenson High Level Bridge over the Tyne, about to take the route through Gateshead West station to join the Team Valley main line.

The standard atlantics were the Class Z (saturated) and Z1 (superheated) and initially ten of each were built by the North British Locomotive Co in 1911 at a cost of £4,485 each. Dynamometer car trials between the two versions commenced on 29 August 1911 and above is 709, fitted with an indicator shelter and telephone cables to the dynamometer car, standing at York awaiting its return working to Newcastle.

The largest NER passenger engines were the pacifics, of which two were built before the grouping of 1923, followed by a further three in 1924. No 2402 was the first of the LNER built engines and it is seen here outside the paint shop at Darlington works. Unusually the three LNER engines were not fitted with Westinghouse brakes when built, but the absence of this was soon felt and they were fitted with Westinghouse pumps within the space of a few months.

Another Royal train brought A4 60028 to the York-Scarborough line on 8 June 1961, seen here near Strensall on the return working from Malton to Kings Cross, after the wedding of the Duke of Kent. Two special trains for guests were also worked by A4 engines.

LOCOMOTIVE DEVELOPMENT

Locomotion No 1 was by no means the first steam locomotive in north eastern England. It was the first steam engine to work a public railway, but steam traction had been in use on a small scale at various collieries for some years before *Locomotion No* 1 appeared in 1825.

From 1857 the engine stood on a stone plinth outside Darlington North Road station, until removed to Bank Top station in 1892. Here it is shown on the original site, chained to the rails! The figure by the leading wheel is in Stockton & Darlington uniform and the photograph was probably taken in the 1860s.

Billy was another Stephenson engine, built about 1830 for use on colliery lines, and it possibly worked until 1880 at Killingworth Colliery. It was then presented to Newcastle Corporation by Sir Charles Mark Palmer and placed on a pedestal at the north end of the High Level Bridge, where it stood until 1896. It was then moved under cover at the recently extended Central station at Newcastle, where it remained until 1945. Finally it was moved to the Science Museum on the Town Moor at Newcastle, where it still stands.

In its growth the NER absorbed what few competitors there were in its territory. One of these was the West Hartlepool Harbour & Railway Co, and it was this company which built the dock around which the town of West Hartlepool developed. The company was taken over in 1865, and the NER became the owners of some Fossick & Hackworth built locomotives with return tube fireboxes and inclined cylinders, similar to those built by Timothy Hackworth for the Stockton & Darlington. The Hackworth in Fossick & Hackworth was Timothy's brother, Thomas, who with his partner, were haulage contractors to the Stockton & Hartlepool Railway and the Clarence Railway, two constituents of the WHHR. The photograph is believed to have been taken at West Hartlepool shed about 1876.

(Right) The WHHR also had some engines with normal boilers but retaining the inclined cylinders. The development from the locomotive illustrated above can easily be seen from the photograph of 628 (ex WHHR 60) taken in the 1870s.

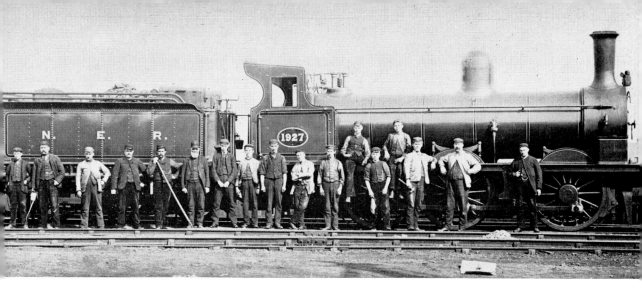

The Blyth & Tyne Railway succumbed to the NER in 1874. Primarily a coal carrying line north of the Tyne, it considered passengers a nuisance! Its locomotives, with their distinctive cabs, were a sturdy breed and 1927 (originally 8 and later 1719) built in 1867 was sold by the NER in 1907 for £600. It was resold to the Seaham Harbour Dock Co and continued to run for a further twenty years as their *Ajax*. The cab was later transferred to another Seaham engine and was found rusting away at Seaham in the 1950s: it was then taken into the custody of the BR Curator of Historical Relics—perhaps some day this sole surviving relic of the Blyth & Tyne will appear on display.

(Right) No 2269 was a 2-4-0T from the Londonderry Railway between Seaham and Sunderland. The line was taken over by the NER in 1900 and incorporated into the new coast route from West Hartlepool to Sunderland. Some of the Londonderry engines strayed from their native heath and 2269 is seen on station pilot duties at Scarborough early in the century.

LOCOMOTIVE WORKS

The three NER locomotive works that survived into the twentieth century were those at York, Gateshead and Darlington. Because of its cramped position and lack of space for expansion the works at York were closed in 1905.

This view shows No 1 erecting shop. The adjoining No 2 shop is now the Eastern Region gymnasium, in which are held table tennis and boxing tournaments.

Gateshead works managed to remain open until 1932, although the construction of new locomotives ceased in 1910. Here again, the trouble was lack of space for expansion. The works reopened in World War II to carry out repairs but closed again in 1959. The photograph was taken in 1906 and shows a number of Class S 4-6-0 engines under construction.

At Darlington (opened in 1863) there was plenty of room and a fine new erecting shop was brought into use in 1903. Here the engines were placed transversely across the shop in three ranks and up to 76 engines could be accommodated. The above photograph shows the shop about 1910.

The new erecting shop remained in use until North Road closed in 1966. This view was taken in 1952.

In 1900 Class S 4-6-0 2006 was sent to the Paris Exhibition (via Hull) and received a gold medal. A plate commemorating this event was carried on each side of the engine, together with replicas of the obverse and reverse of the medal in small glass-fronted cases. These replicas and the plates are now in the Railway Museum at York.

(Below left) The Seaham Harbour Dock Co purchased two NER Class 964 0-6-0 ST (complete with numberplates) and the new owners made their own nameplates by grinding down the NER numerals and then rivetting on to the plate the letters for the name. On the plates on *Milo* the figures were not completely removed and the NER number remained visible beneath the name. (Below right) Electric locomotive 5 retained its NER livery and numberplate until BR days.

LOCOMOTIVE SHEDS
AND THEIR FACILITIES

NER engine sheds varied from small dark buildings to large spacious roundhouses and it is amazing how the locomotives were kept clean and in running order considering the conditions under which the staff had to work. The photograph above shows two spotless Class A 2-4-2T at Whitby about 1910.

The largest NER shed was Hull Dairycoates, with an allocation of 150 engines. Until extensions were completed in 1916 many of the engines had to stand outside, as shown in this 1913 photograph. A sole Lancashire & Yorkshire visitor can be seen on the left.

The last new shed to be built for steam in the north east was at Thornaby (between Stockton and Middlesbrough) and opened in 1958. In addition to a straight shed (above) there was a particularly fine and spacious roundhouse to follow the traditional North Eastern and Stockton & Darlington circular sheds (below). Now, of course, steam locomotives have disappeared from the north eastern BR scene and the shed is used solely by diesel locomotives.

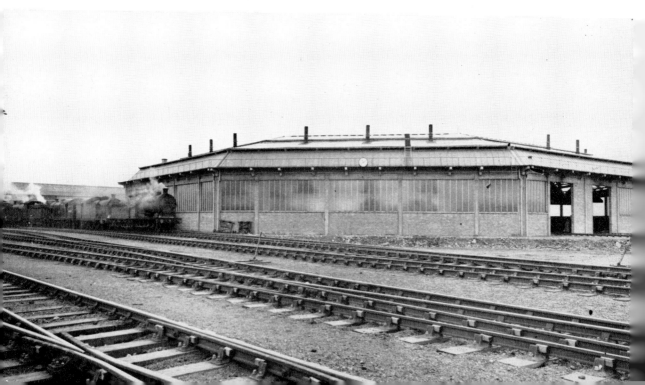

Gateshead was also a large shed with a number of adjoining roundhouses and in the 1950s it was rebuilt with a new roof (above). Later, the turntables and radiating roads were removed and the building converted to a straight shed for diesel locomotives (below).

Coaling facilities provided normally comprised a coal stage, on to which the loaded coal wagons were shunted. The coal was then shovelled into small wheeled tubs which were run across the stage and tipped either direct, or down a chute, on to the tender. Fletcher 2-4-0 853 is shown at the old York coaling stage, demolished about 1914 to make way for extensions to the shed. A new coaling stage was erected in the yard and this remained in use until the mechanical coaling plant was installed in the 1930s.

At some sheds a steam crane was used to hoist the tubs above the tender or bunker: an end door on the tub was then opened and the coal tipped out where required. This method was employed at Malton (left) until the shed closed in 1963.

30

Hull Dairycoates had an early form of mechanical coaling plant installed in 1916 and this remained in use for exactly fifty years (below).

The plant at Neville Hill was of the pattern favoured by the LNER and was erected in 1932 (right).

Darlington shed was completely rebuilt in 1939 and a new coaling plant brought into use. This was demolished in 1967.

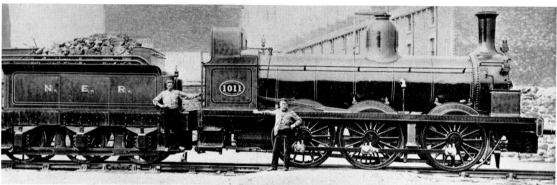

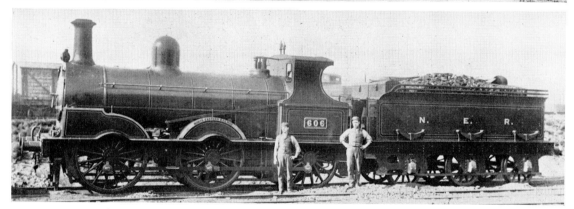

THE GOODS ENGINES, WAGONS AND VANS

To work the large amount of freight and mineral traffic, the NER maintained a large fleet of 0-6-0 engines. Out of the 2,164 engines at 1 January 1923, 533 were of this type, including a number of Fletcher 398 class introduced in 1874. No 1389 in 'Worsdellised' condition is seen at the old Bank Top shed at Darlington c 1895 (top).

Also extant at grouping was a single example of the Stockton & Darlington long-boilered 0-6-0, but 1011 shown here was scrapped in 1908 from Waskerley shed (centre).

McDonnell introduced his 0-6-0 design in 1883 and 606 (bottom) is seen here in original condition, with McDonnell chimney, left hand drive, and sloping smokebox front.

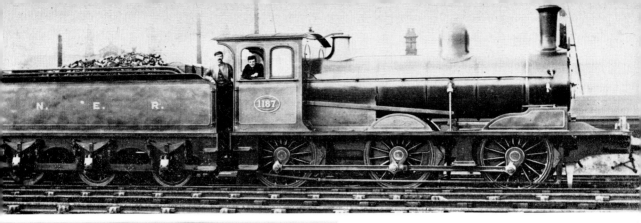

Perhaps the most successful NER 0-6-0 design was T. W. Worsdell's Class C (compound) and C1 (simple) introduced in 1886. 171 compounds and 30 simples were built but all the compounds were rebuilt to Class C1 by Wilson Worsdell. Many were later fitted with automatic brakes and put in a lot of work on passenger trains. The last was not withdrawn until 1962. No 1187 (top) was fitted with extended frames to accommodate piston tail rods.

The largest NER 0-6-0s were those with 5 ft 6 in diameter boilers and classified P2 and P3, built between 1904 and 1923. No 65894, which has been purchased for preservation, is seen on Seaton Bank, south of Sunderland, in October 1966 (centre).

The LNER also produced a design with a 5 ft 6 in boiler . . . the J39 class, many of which were built at Darlington works. Here is 1470 on a goods on the east coast main line at Croft Spa (bottom).

33

The mineral wagons hauled by the 0-6-0 engines were usually built by the NER in their own shops and private owners' wagons were not very common in the north east. The large twenty ton hopper wagons are well known, and illustrated (top) is a Central Division wagon lettered 'To work between Hedley Hope and Newport'.

A large amount of coke was carried between Durham and Cumberland, over the Stainmore line, the one-time South Durham & Lancashire Union Railway. Illustrated (centre) is a railed wagon with ten and a half ton capacity.

All-metal forty ton hopper wagons were built by contractors and used mainly between Ashington and Blyth, where the coal was 'teemed' into ships berthed at staiths (bottom).

For express goods services between large centres, and also for 'road' traffic the NER used a number of double bogie vehicles. No 106340 was built in 1907.

It was usual for railways to carry a stock of special wagons for unusual traffic and here *Meteor* is mounted on a twelve ton agricultural wagon. The engine was a product of Black, Hawthorn & Co of Gateshead and it was on its way to Knight, Bevan & Spurge of Northfleet, Kent, in 1893. Gauge 2 ft 8½ in.

For many years the North Eastern preferred bird-cage lookouts on its brake vans but here are two old vans, and one of the later pattern with side duckets for the guard.

ROAD VEHICLES—GOODS

To deliver the goods traffic the NER, as with all other companies before the petrol age, relied on horses. Here are sixteen heavy horses and their carters outside the goods station at Scarborough.

In 1904 the North Eastern started using a steam lurry (*sic*) for country goods delivery services. This is a Straker of 5 tons capacity.

Shortly afterwards petrol vans were introduced for parcels delivery.

In the 1930s came the ubiquitous mechanical horse, seen here double-heading a tow-motor (as used for shunting on the docks at Hull). The engine on the low trailer is Class Y8 0-4-0T 559 *en route* in 1940 from Patrington to the isolated military railway at Spurn Head.

ROAD VEHICLES—PASSENGER

The NER introduced passenger road services in 1903, only a few days after the Great Western Railway, and for the original Beverley to Brandesburton service purchased three Stirling buses. Here are two of them in the village of Beeford. The shop on the right still stands, although the adjoining cottages have been demolished, and the bus service through the village is now provided by the East Yorkshire Motor Services.

In 1905 the NER started using char-a-bancs on tours from the station yards at Bridlington, Harrogate and Scarborough. Illustrated is BT 362 about to set off for Forge Valley, a beauty spot just outside Scarborough.

Some of the char-a-bancs were fitted with interchangeable bodies and could be used for goods traffic in the winter months. However, BT 368 was rebuilt with an early form of double-deck body.

The NER also had an extensive bus network around Durham City, using mainly Leyland buses. In an effort to provide similar facilities by rail in the York area one of the Durham buses was converted to run on rails. It could be driven from either end (the photograph above is from the rear) and it took part in the Railway Centenary Procession in July 1925, in which it is seen approaching Urlay Nook level crossing. It was destroyed by fire in November 1926.

RAILCARS—PETROL

The first experiments with internal combustion engined railcars were in 1903, when the NER built two petrol-electric bogie vehicles (above). These were intended for use between West Hartlepool and Hartlepool, but they actually commenced working between Scarborough and Filey in August 1904. During the winter months they worked between Billingham and Port Clarence before being transferred to Selby in 1908 to work the Cawood branch.

The NER also built some small petrol cars for use by the Company's officers on visits of inspection. No 3711 was built in 1908 and was the smallest: two larger cars were built in 1912.

Ordered by the North Eastern but not completed until LNER days was 2105Y, a six-wheeled car with two wheels at one end and a bogie at the other. This car worked in the York area, running to Copmanthorpe, Strensall and Poppleton, but it did little work after the stations on the Scarborough branch were closed in 1930 and the car was scrapped in 1934.

600 & 1,500 VOLTS

Electric traction was introduced on the lines north of the River Tyne as early as March 1904. At first it was impossible to work a circular service as there was no connection between the main line at Manors and the old Blyth & Tyne station at New Bridge Street. However, this link was inserted in 1909 but even then circular working was not introduced, and it did not commence to operate until 1917.

The opening day scene shows the first train from New Bridge Street standing preparing for departure, with NER officials and guests on the platform. The gentleman facing the camera on the left is George Stegmann Gibb, the NER General Manager, who was knighted in the same year as the photograph was taken.

42

In 1918 a disastrous fire occurred at the NER electric car sheds at Heaton in which thirty-four vehicles were destroyed and many damaged. Replacement cars were built and it was these which were modernised in 1938 for use on the newly electrified South Shields line. The illustration shows a six car train of the rebuilt stock in the red and cream livery adopted at that time (above).

Also in 1938 the whole of the North Tyneside electric stock was replaced by articulated twins built by Metro-Cammell. Here is E29114E+E29314E in BR green livery (below).

In conjunction with the North Tyneside electrification the steeply graded Quayside branch was converted for electric traction and two locomotives were built for the line, much of which is in tunnel. These were numbered 1 and 2 and initially they carried CLASS ELECTRIC 1 on the buffer beams. A bow collector was originally fitted but this was soon replaced by a pantograph on the cab roof.

A special brake van with extra sanding facilities was provided for the branch and here is the van attached to 26500 (originally 1) at the Quayside Yard end of the branch in September 1957.

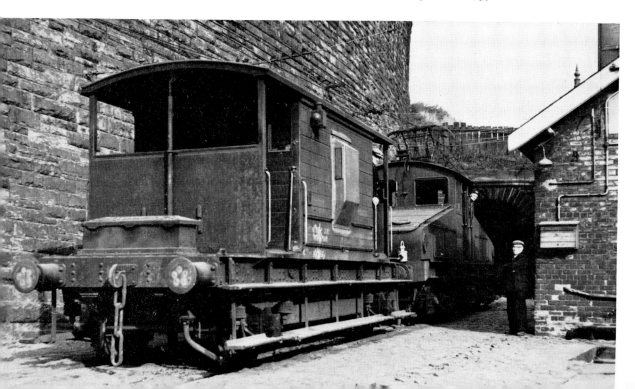

The Shildon-Newport electrified system was inaugurated in 1914 using 1,500v dc, for which ten locomotives were built at Darlington. The gradient was falling in favour of the loaded trains running towards Newport and here is 11 on a load of coke. The electric equipment was abandoned in 1935 and the locomotives placed in store for a further fifteen years before being scrapped.

Extensive overhead equipment was necessary at the Newport end and this view of Erimus Yard shows the forest of supports and wires, with a Class T 0-8-0 on the right.

PASSENGER LOCOMOTIVES AND COACHES

For passenger traffic the NER owned a number of 2-4-0s, of which the most popular were those introduced by Edward Fletcher in 1872, and the Tennants of 1885. The latter were designed by a committee under the chairmanship of Henry Tennant, although it seems certain that most of the work was done by Wilson Worsdell, who later became Locomotive Superintendent of the company. Wilson Worsdell's brother, Thomas William, moved from the Great Eastern to the North Eastern in 1885 and he designed a couple of compound 2-4-0s of Class D, which were later rebuilt with bogies and reclassified F.

The illustrations show:

(top) Fletcher 2-4-0 927 (Class 901) in T. W. Worsdell's livery c 1890.

(centre) Tennant 1469 in Wilson Worsdell's livery.

(bottom) Class D 1324 as built but in Wilson Worsdell's livery c 1895.

The Stockton & Darlington was early in the field with 4-4-0s and used them on the Darlington-Kirkby Stephen-Tebay line over Stainmore Summit from 1861. Before they ordered these engines the company was offered a 4-4-0 with which to run trials by Robert Stephenson & Co. The top illustration shows this trial engine at Shildon.

Wilson Worsdell's first 4-4-0 design appeared in 1892 and consisted of twenty Class M1 engines 1620-39. These took part in the 1895 races and 1621 is now preserved in the Railway Museum at York. The centre illustration shows 1627 at the east end of Newcastle Central in 1894, when the station was being extended.

The final design of 4-4-0 used in the north east was the D49, introduced in 1927 and designed by Gresley. Later engines were fitted with rotary cam operated poppet valves and named after hunts. For this reason the nameplates were surmounted by a cast brass running fox. The lower illustration shows 214 *The Atherstone* built in 1934.

The North Eastern started building bogie stock in quantity in 1896 and for ten years concentrated on vehicles with clerestory roofs before changing over to the elliptical roof. Most of the clerestory roof stock had separate compartments but the above illustration shows an open composite, one of four built in 1904.

A familiar sight between 1905 and 1925 were the autocars already mentioned. An unusual feature was the provision of circular spectacles in the driving compartments. Illustrated below is a two-coach autocar, with the engine in the centre, used on the Hull and Beverley service.

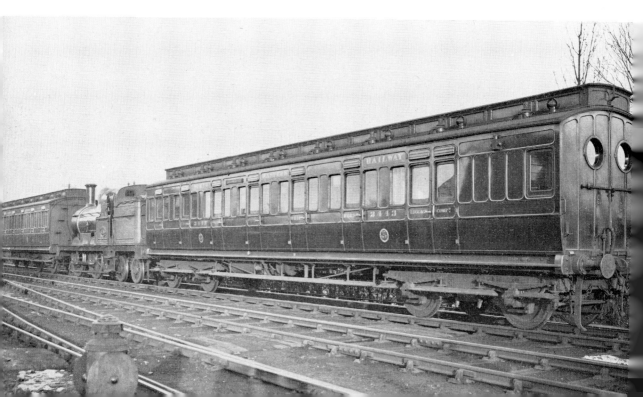

In 1906 the NER changed to the elliptical roof and the above illustration shows 57, a brake third built in 1907 for excursion traffic. Gas was still being used for lighting, but later vehicles to the same design were fitted with electric lighting, which increased the weight from 23 tons 5 cwt to 24 tons 15 cwt. Standard lengths over headstocks were 49 ft 0 in and 52 ft 0 in, although some 45 ft 0 in coaches were built for use in the Whitby area.

In June 1908 some trains of handsome corridor stock appeared for use on the Newcastle-Liverpool services. The majority of the stock was eight-wheeled and 52 ft 0 in over headstocks, but the magnificent dining cars were twelve-wheeled and 65 ft 6 in over headstocks, weighing 41 tons (below).

A large fleet of six-wheeled coaches was maintained for special traffic and excursions and, in fact, in 1909 there were 939 thirds of one type alone. Club saloons were used between Bridlington and Hull, Scarborough and Hull, and Scarborough and Leeds and 1029, built in 1885, was converted to a Club saloon in March 1911 (above). The interior of these saloons was fitted with armchairs and tables and the occupants normally passed the time by playing cards. Note gas lighting, with cords to pull hoods over the lights (below).

Some of the most interesting and long lived coaches were the official inspection saloons. Latterly these were six or eight-wheeled vehicles, but one four-wheeler remained in use until 1967. This was NER 1173, later LNER 21173 and 900270. For many years it was used by the district engineer at Hull, but when this post became joint with the York district the saloon became spare. It subsequently passed to the gauging section at North Eastern Region HQ until sold in 1967 for private preservation. The view (above) shows the interior, looking towards the glazed end.

Spartan in comparison was the early Tyneside electric stock with rattan seating on reversible seat frames imported from America (below).

TRACKSIDE FEATURES

There was not a great variety in NER noticeboards and most of them appear to date from the turn of the century. They were normally over the signature of the secretaries:

C. N. Wilkinson	1871-1903
R. L. Wedgwood	1904-5
R. F. Dunnell	1905-22

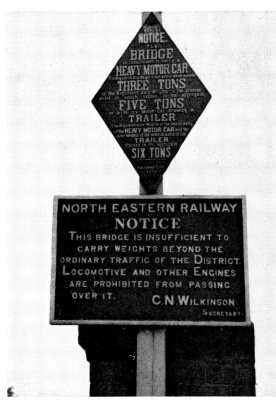

A reminder of the early days of road transport.

In 1905 the whole of the NER system was remeasured and distinctive $\frac{1}{4}$, $\frac{1}{2}$, and $\frac{3}{4}$ mileposts erected.

Many of the stations had a map of the NER system mounted on the wall. This was made up of sixty-four glazed tiles, with a further eight for the heading and forty-eight for the beading. A few of these tile maps are still in existence, although in some cases now covered by a large poster. However, those at Beverley and Whitby can still be seen.

STAFF AND STATIONS

A fine period view of Brough (East Yorkshire) station c 1870. The building was replaced early in this century, when realignment and quadrupling of the tracks took place, but the building still stands adjacent to the down slow line.

The staff at Fence Houses. Note the number of staff employed at this wayside station between Durham and Sunderland. The station was closed to passenger traffic on 4 May 1964 and to goods traffic four weeks later.

York, now the headquarters of the Eastern Region, has a station with five through platforms. The longest of these is 1,692 ft long and can accommodate two trains with ease. Here is an up express arriving at the south end of this platform .   .   .   now No 8 but originally No 4.

The origin of this drawing of a station interior is unknown but it is obviously based on Harrogate.

Some of the stations in the north east are very old and still exist in their original or rebuilt form. One of the latter is Hull Paragon, where what was originally the main frontage of the 1848 building is now used for parcels traffic (right).

The station was extended and a new frontage built in 1904, with the new portico facing on to Paragon Square (below).

In the 1960s the 1904 portico was replaced by an office block but the platforms remained unchanged.

Some stations were replaced at an early date and an unusual sight in gardens at Saltburn is the portico from the original Barnard Castle station. This station became redundant for passengers when the line was extended over the Pennines to Kirkby Stephen and Tebay in 1861 and the portico was purchased by the Saltburn Improvement Co and transported to Saltburn, then in its infancy.

A typical NER station scene but actually photographed early in LNER days. However, little has changed, except that the engine and coaches are lettered LNER and the stationmaster has on a new uniform. The train is a Newcastle-Carlisle express with Class D17/2 1921 at the head.

The LNER erected a few stations to serve new housing estates and one such was on the outskirts of Leeds at Osmondthorpe, between Marsh Lane and Cross Gates. This was opened on 29 September 1930 and here is a Selby-Leeds slow train (with Class D22 1537).

After World War II came Filey Holiday Camp station to serve the Butlin's camp on the East Yorkshire coast. In addition to the station three new signal boxes were provided, together with a triangular layout. It was at the end of platform 3 that K3 61846 hit the buffers at speed and jumped on to the platform.

Extensive sidings were provided by the North Eastern at their larger centres. At Hull, in addition to local goods traffic, there was import and export traffic to be handled and sorted, and large groups of sidings were laid down, particularly on the west side of the city. The above view, looking east, shows the Outward Yard, with Dairycoates engine shed and coaling plant in the left background.

The NER would also provide a siding to serve a single farm if it was remote from a station. These sidings, which were scattered throughout the system, were usually on country branch lines but did also occur on the main line as at Manor House (between Thirsk and Otterington). This siding was not closed until 1964. It was the site of the famous collision of 1892 when nine passengers and a guard were killed.

Stationmaster First Class in frock coat issued to stationmasters at Durham, Darlington, Saltburn, Malton, Tynemouth and Ferryhill, and assistant stationmasters at Newcastle and York.

Policeman in his summer style uniform.

NER staff were well supplied with uniforms and full details were laid down as to their entitlement. Specifications for each type of suit, coat and cap were issued in a glossy volume, with illustrations of the various items, down to the various sizes and grades of metal buttons. This is a goods guard.

Off duty (and sometimes on) many railwaymen made for the 'local' and public houses with a railway connection in their title are to be found throughout the country. Two in the north east are the *Railway Hotel* at Spennymoor (above) which uses the Newcastle & Carlisle locomotive *Comet* for its sign, and the *Stanhope & Tyne Railway Inn* (below) at Annfield Plain. Although the Stanhope & Tyne Railway lost its identity well over a century ago, the name still persists.

INCLINES

The Stanhope & Tyne was an early line built to transport limestone and coal from the Stanhope and Consett area to the mouth of the Tyne at South Shields. A few stretches were worked by locomotives but the majority of the line was on inclines, which were either self-acting or winding engine. To reach the floor of the Team Valley four inclines were necessary on the west side, the Loud, Stanley, Eden Hill and Waldridge banks, and although Loud Bank was replaced by a locomotive worked line in the 1880s the others continued to work for many years. In fact, Waldridge Incline is still in operation, but since 1966 has been operated by a diesel-electric locomotive and rope-working abandoned.

The historic Tanfield branch on the outskirts of Gateshead was also worked by a series of inclines, some of which lasted until well into British Railways' days. One of these was Bakers Bank, where operation was made difficult by a level crossing at the summit. Note the 'kips' on either side used by the ascending wagons: once they were over the crest the wagons coasted to safety.

The Durham & Sunderland Railway was another hilly line originally worked solely by winding engines and gravity. Change to locomotive haulage was made about 1860, but the banks still called for hard locomotive work a century later. A typical scene of the 1960s shows a Newcastle-Kings Cross train diverted up Seaton Bank on a Sunday in May 1961, with V3 67687 assisting A3 60050 *Persimmon* on the climb.

Later lines were built to use locomotives from the outset and one of the steepest was the Scarborough & Whitby Railway opened in 1885. This involved a long climb at 1 in 39 and normally assistance was provided with trains of over five coaches. Here is a scenic excursion climbing the bank with A8 69865 assisting B1 61115 in June 1955.

An even later line was the Scarborough, Bridlington & West Riding Junction Railway opened in 1890. This company did not fulfil its title and built only the link between Market Weighton and Driffield. For many years this proved a useful route for passenger traffic from the West Riding to the resorts of Bridlington and Scarborough but it involved climbing Enthorpe Bank; four miles at 1 in 95 and 1 in 100. Here is B16/3 61468 piloting a Class 5 4-6-0.

VIADUCTS AND BRIDGES

The north east is particularly rich in bridges, made necessary by the hilly nature of much of the country. Many of them were built of stone or metal from the outset and wooden bridges were never very common in the north east. County Durham is fortunate in having the first stone railway bridge . . . the Causey Arch, built in 1727 to carry a colliery line. It has long been disused for this purpose but this fine bridge still stands and carries a footpath across the gorge. It is now preserved as an Ancient Monument and it is an outstanding tribute to the work of the early railway engineers.

The Durham Junction Railway formed a small but important link in the chain of railways from London to the Tyne, connecting with the Newcastle & Darlington Junction at Rainton and with the Stanhope & Tyne (later Pontop & South Shields) at Washington. It was less than five miles long, but in this length included the magnificent Victoria Bridge across the Wear: it was so called because of the last stone which was laid on the day of Queen Victoria's coronation in June 1838. Until the Team Valley route was opened the bridge was used by all east coast trains between London and Edinburgh.

67

The River Ouse at Selby was bridged by rail in 1840 when the Hull & Selby was opened. With the opening of the York-Selby and Selby-Shaftholme links in the 1870s Selby found itself on the main line. The original bascule bridge sufficed until 1891, when the present swing bridge was opened slightly downstream.

The lower picture looks northwards across the new bridge, with the gauntletted down main and down slow on the left. The up tracks were similarly laid until spring points were installed on the north side of the bridge. Now the gauntletting on the down tracks has also been removed with the installation of power operated points at the far side. The derelict signal box on the extreme left of the picture is on the course of the line across the old bridge.

Notable metal viaducts were constructed on the South Durham & Lancashire Union Railway between Barnard Castle and Tebay, and on the Scarborough, Whitby, Redcar & Middlesbrough Union line between Whitby and Loftus. In both cases these were built up of tubular columns but they have all been demolished in the last ten years. The most notable were Belah and Deepdale, between Barnard Castle and Kirkby Stephen, both built by Gilkes Wilson & Co to the designs of Thomas Bouch, the designer of the ill-fated Tay Bridge. The illustration shows Deepdale Viaduct under construction. Note the incline railway for conveying materials down the valley side, and also the height of the man in front of the base of the pier in the foreground.

Belah (above) was of similar construction and in the 1950s, after forty years of severe weight restrictions, these were relaxed by BR, allowing double-headed trains to be worked over to Blackpool on summer Saturdays. However, the principal traffic was for many years coke going westwards and iron ore going eastwards.

Staithes (below) was very near the coast and for safety reasons had a wind gauge. When the force of the wind reached danger level a bell rang in the signal box and traffic was suspended until the gale abated. The line over the bridge was closed in 1958 and the viaduct was demolished two years later.

To turn to the smaller bridges, one of the first stone skew bridges was on the Haggerleases branch of the Stockton & Darlington, opened in 1830. This was a novelty at the time and it was predicted that it would not stand to carry its own weight, never mind loaded mineral trains. In fact it was used by rail traffic until 1963.

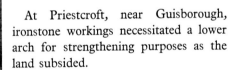

At Priestcroft, near Guisborough, ironstone workings necessitated a lower arch for strengthening purposes as the land subsided.

At Kirby Moorside part of the closed branch to Pickering has been converted to a road. The original railway bridge has been used for the road but more than doubled in width, with the old part of the bridge still retaining its NER bridge numberplate.

71

Subsidence has long been a problem in mining areas and Kilton Viaduct, (opened in 1867), in the midst of the Cleveland ironstone workings became unsafe some forty years later and it was buried under thousands of tons of spoil from the nearby mines, thus converting it into an embankment. As such it still stands but it is now disused. The photograph also shows the Skinningrove zig-zag, with a reversing neck passing under the near end of the viaduct.

There were some notable timber viaducts between Newcastle and North Shields, the largest being across the Ouseburn valley at Newcastle, and across Willington Dene, near North Shields. These were of laminated form and they attracted a lot of attention when new. Both viaducts were rebuilt in metal a century ago, a most unusual feature being the similarity in appearance between the original viaducts and their replacements. The illustration shows a two-car electric train on Willington Dene viaduct.

Many of the rivers of the north form county boundaries, although to be strictly correct the boundary is down the centre line of the river. In the centre of the King Edward Bridge over the Tyne the exact boundary is marked by two signs denoting Northumberland to the north and County Durham to the south (above).

The North Eastern main line terminated with a fine stone viaduct across the Tweed at Berwick, officially known as the Royal Border Bridge although the England/Scotland border is a few miles to the north. The bridge, opened in 1850 by Queen Victoria, has 28 arches each 61 ft 6 in span, with a total length of 2,160 ft and a maximum height of 126 ft 6 in.

The viaduct straddling the City of Durham was built to carry the Bishop Auckland branch but later became part of the east coast main line. The Cathedral makes a fine backdrop to the view from the train as it slowly crosses the bridge, with the bustling streets of the city spread out below.

Not far away, at Ushaw Moor on the Waterhouses branch, stood a pair of timber viaducts: however, these had been rebuilt and were not of great antiquity. After the closure of the branch the viaducts were dismantled in 1966.

TUNNELS

There were some long and notable tunnels in the north east, although often in out-of-the-way places and not well known. Some of them have a claim to fame because of their historic associations and, in fact, two of the tunnels pictured have been disused for more than a century.

The Whitby & Pickering Railway was originally horse worked and at Grosmont a tunnel was built to accommodate such traffic. Steam locomotives were introduced on the line in 1847 and for these a full sized tunnel had to be built alongside the original. Fortunately the redundant horse tunnel was allowed to remain and has since been used to give access to some cottages.

A re-arrangement of the lines at Harrogate in 1862 meant the abandoning of Brunswick station and also the tunnel leading to it. However, the tunnel still remains and parts of it were used as an air raid shelter in World War II.

Also abandoned now is Burdale Tunnel between Malton and Driffield, through the chalk Yorkshire Wolds. A few yards short of a mile in length this was the major engineering work on the little Malton & Driffield Railway opened in 1853.

Brotherton tunnel, on the Y & NM Burton Salmon-Knottingley branch, was shortened in 1952, when some 200 yds were removed from the southern end. Most of this end of the tunnel was covered only with a thin layer of earth and had been provided to hide the trains from nearby Byram Hall.

The MR 2-4-0 is on a York-Sheffield train via the S & K Joint line, which commences a mile south of this viewpoint. The cottage on the extreme right still stands but the portal is now 215 yds further north.

Farnley tunnel, near Corbridge (below) was abandoned in 1960 when it was replaced by a cutting on a new alignment. The view shows the western portal, with work on the cutting in progress and the river Tyne in the background.

NOTABLE JUNCTIONS

There were some notable junctions too: what railway enthusiast interested in the east coast route has not heard of Shaftholme Junction, where the Great Northern and the North Eastern joined north of Doncaster? This enabled the two English east coast partners to become independent of the Lancashire & Yorkshire, whose metals they had used as far as Knottingley. The small box at Shaftholme Junction was a famous timing point but it was replaced by a new box when the main line was realigned in 1958. Here is the up Flying Scotsman passing the old box in 1951 (above).

The other end of the link to Shaftholme was at Chaloner Whin, two miles south of York. Here we are looking along the four track section to Church Fenton, with the main line to Selby and Shaftholme Junction bearing away left. The signal box was demolished in 1951 when colour light signals were inaugurated.

78

The famous crossing at the east end of Newcastle Central has been extensively photographed, particularly from the Castle keep, which stands in the fork of the lines to the north and across the High Level Bridge. This vantage point gives an excellent view of the layout and working and above we see a train leaving Platform 5 and passing on to the High Level Bridge: a G5 0-4-4T is blowing off awaiting a signal; a North Tyneside electric train is entering Platform 3, and a J71 or J72 0-6-0T pilot stands on the right.

In the lower view a pacific is backing down; B1 61020 *Gemsbok* arrives on an empty coaching stock train, whilst K1 62059 passes on a goods.

North of Newcastle the old Blyth & Tyne route from Manors ran on the west side of the main line before crossing it near Benton to reach Backworth and Monkseaton. This route formed part of the electric circle and here we see an eastbound electric train crossing above the main line.

Below, on the south side of the Tyne, is Pontop Crossing, where the Gateshead-Sunderland line is crossed on the level by the old Stanhope & Tyne. Until recently the latter was used by the Consett ore trains but these have now been diverted via Gateshead and only NCB coal trains pass over the crossing from north to south, although the Gateshead-Sunderland line is heavily used.

SIGNALS AND SIGNALLING

The North Eastern has long been noted for the number of signals it used to control trains. At York and Newcastle there were forests of signals, most of which were supplied by Messrs McKenzie & Holland of Worcester. The largest manual box was Locomotive Yard at York, with 295 levers (above) opened in June 1909 and replaced by an all-electric box in 1951. Thirsk (below) was one of the first electric boxes and was opened in November 1933 in connection with main line improvements.

At many places boxes supported on a girder framework were used. This one at Coxhoe Junction was unusual in that it controlled traffic on two levels.

At other sites where space was at a premium overhanging boxes were used, either with a single-sided overhang as at Wellfield (below), or with a double overhang as at Grosmont (see page 86).

82

For single line branches various types of control were used . . . staff and ticket; electric tablet; electric key token, and latterly transient track circuits. Hand exchanges by means of a pouch and loop still persist, although the line through Slingsby, on which the Newcastle-Scarborough summer Saturdays train is running (right) has since been lifted.

An experimental form of signalling tried between Knaresborough and Pilmoor in the 1930s necessitated a powerful headlamp on the engine to pick out the various reflector studded signals (left).

An early form of train control was installed at Middlesbrough. It covered the various ironworks on Tees-side and the iron mines in nearby Cleveland as far as Battersby and Brotton (below).

ACCIDENTS . . . AND THEIR PREVENTION

The Raven fog signalling apparatus was extensively used on the NER, usually to indicate to the driver the position of the distant signal. A trip lever in the four foot struck a pendulum lever on the engine if the signal was at caution: this caused a whistle to blow in the engine cab and the brakes to be partially applied unless cancelled by the driver. The above illustration shows the trip levers in the four foot. Below left is the pendulum lever about to strike the trip lever, and below right is a more sophisticated system, using electrical instead of mechanical operation. In addition to indicating the position of the signals this apparatus also indicated which of up to four routes the train was signalled to take.

Unfortunately, the various safeguards did not always prevent accidents, and the Tweedmouth crew were killed when they ran through signals and collided with the rear of a freight train standing at Darlington in November 1910.

Another serious collision occurred within a few yards in 1928, when an excursion returning from Scarborough to Newcastle collided with the engine of a parcels train which was carrying out shunting operations.

SNOW ON THE LINE

Snow has always been a hazard on the railways of the north east, particularly in the wild Pennine uplands and on the Yorkshire Moors. Learning from experience, the NER built a fleet of large, heavy snowploughs, which were usually marshalled in pairs facing in opposite directions, with one, two, or even three locomotives between them. These could move deep drifts, although on occasions trouble occurred due to the snow building up under the blade of the plough, thus lifting the front wheels off the rails.

Above is a view of two ploughs, with a pair of Q6 0-8-0 between. (Below) Platforms had to be cleared of snow for passengers and a practical hand plough was used for this purpose at Grosmont.

The line which suffered most was over Stainmore Summit and often trains became stuck fast in the snow and had to be abandoned. In 1947 one engine remained embedded for almost two months before it could be rescued.

SHIPS AND SHIPPING

The North Eastern had large dock interests. These arose in various ways: in some cases the docks were built by a railway company and taken over with that company, such as the West Hartlepool Harbour & Railway, and the Hull & Barnsley Railway. In others the NER purchased the dock system, as at Hull in 1893. At Sunderland, however, the docks were built by the Sunderland Dock Co, and although the company was sponsored by various railway companies (behind which stood George Hudson) the docks never did become railway property. Nevertheless, the docks were opened by George Hudson in June 1850, and the picture shows the opening ceremony.

Peculiar to north eastern England were the coal staiths—raised wooden gantries from which the coal was tipped direct into the holds of ships. Some of these staiths were erected as late as the 1920s. Illustrated are Dunston Staiths.

As the ship was loaded and settled in the water the coal had further to fall and it suffered severe breakage. To overcome this various types of anti-breakage appliances were used to lower the coal into the holds and two types can be seen here. The two gantries each carry one loader and another pattern is suspended from the crane.

The NER operated cargo and passenger steamers between Hull and the Continent through the Hull & Holland Steamship Service Joint Committee, and also in conjunction with Thomas Wilson & Co Ltd. The fleet of the former was augmented when the NER became a partner and four new vessels were acquired: later the LNER added the *Melrose Abbey* (above).

Another familiar sight on the Humber were the Hull-New Holland ferries: these were shallow-draught paddle steamers for crossing the treacherous sandbanks of the river. This service descended from the Manchester, Sheffield & Lincolnshire Railway, through the Great Central and LNER to BR and is still in operation. In 1934 the LNER obtained two new vessels—the *Wingfield Castle* and the *Tattershall Castle*: the latter is illustrated.

LOCOMOTIVE BUILDERS

The NER and LNER were usually willing to allow north country locomotive builders to carry out trials on their lines. As early as 1872 Manning, Wardle & Co were permitted to try out a Fell locomotive destined for Brazil on the Goathland incline. In this case, however, the special track had to be laid at the expense of the builders of the engine.

Armstrong Whitworths of Newcastle on Tyne made an early attempt to enter the diesel locomotive market and tried out various railcars and locomotives on the LNER. Here is an 880 hp locomotive at Blaydon.

Another famous Leeds firm, Kitson & Co, carried out extensive trials over LNER metals with the Kitson-Still steam and diesel locomotive, seen here at Beverley in 1932.

Locomotive building on Tyneside was mainly in the hands of Robert Stephenson & Co and R. & W. Hawthorn, although there were a number of smaller firms building locomotives in the nineteenth century. R. & W. Hawthorn later became part of the Hawthorn Leslie combine and produced for the LNER in 1925/6 thirteen splendid 4-6-2T of Class A5.

The forerunners of Kitson & Co   .   .   .   Kitson, Thompson & Hewitson   .   .   . built a 2-2-2WT for display at the Great Exhibition in 1851, and in the following year this was purchased by the Leeds Northern Railway. The engine, which carried the name *Aerolite*, was destroyed in a collision in 1868 but the name was handed down to its successors, one of which can be seen in the Railway Museum at York. There, too, are the builders' plate and nameplate from the original engine.

NAMING CEREMONIES

For many years *Aerolite* was the only named engine on the NER. However, the LNER favoured names for its larger locomotives, many of which were named after Regiments or Public Schools. A naming ceremony was often held and V2 4818 was named *St Peter's School* at York in 1939.

Twenty years later 60964 of the same class was named *Durham Light Infantry* at a ceremony held at Durham station. Here the Colonel of the Regiment unveils the nameplate.

INDUSTRIAL AND LIGHT RAILWAYS

Privately owned docks served by privately owned railways appeared in the north east and a typical example was Seaham Harbour, built to handle the coal produced by the Londonderry family pits in County Durham. For many years, due to the need for economy, the company used ancient locomotives and illustrated below is a 0-4-0ST on harbour wall repair works. Built by Lewin, the exact date of the locomotive is uncertain, but it was built some time between 1860 and 1870. Note the chaldron wagons at the rear of the train.

Mars, also of the Seaham Harbour Co, was originally a North Eastern Class 964 0-6-0ST, sold out of service in 1908. This engine continued to work at Seaham until 1963, although the class disappeared from the North Eastern as long ago as 1909.

Some of the colliery companies in Durham and Northumberland ran passenger services for their employees, using coaching stock purchased from main line railway companies. One of these systems was at Ashington, where a number of ex-NER coaches were in use. The photograph was taken in 1967 on the occasion of a special train over the line.

In another category was the military railway at Spurn, at the mouth of the Humber. This conveyed stores and military personnel only. The view from the lighthouse, looking east, shows Spurn Point, with the North Sea on one side (left) and the River Humber on the other (right).

The service on the Spurn Military Railway was at one time worked by the locomotive *Kenyon* a 2-4-0T. Later a Hudswell Clarke petrol railcar was used.

Light railways were few and far between in North Eastern territory and those that were built were usually small systems, often with only one engine and a handful of coaches. Usually they owed their existence to the fact that the towns and villages they served had been neglected by the main line company.

The Easingwold Railway left the east coast main line at Alne, eleven miles north of York: it was opened in 1891 and closed in 1957, although passenger traffic ceased in 1948. It remained an independent company throughout.

The Cawood, Wistow & Selby, on the other hand, was soon taken over by the NER after its opening in 1897. Passenger services ceased in 1930 but freight traffic continued until 1960.

The North Sunderland Railway also connected with the east coast main line, at Chathill, forty-six miles north of Newcastle. It too remained independent but was latterly worked by a steam locomotive hired from BR. It was opened in 1898 and closed in 1951.

The Derwent Valley Light Railway has managed to survive until the present day, although its line, which originally ran from York to Cliff Common, has had to be truncated as an economy measure. An earlier attempt to economise in traction costs was made in the 1920s, when a Sentinel geared steam locomotive was purchased, and also a twin Ford rail-bus set. The latter was borrowed by the LNER during the General Strike of 1926 and was used in the Harrogate area. It is seen here at Knaresborough.

The Nidd Valley Light Railway was intended to convey men and materials to the huge reservoirs under construction for Bradford Corporation at the head of Nidderdale. To gain a foothold in the valley the Corporation purchased the powers of a previously authorised light railway and because of this were compelled to run a public passenger service over part of their line, between Pateley Bridge and Lofthouse. At first the passenger service was worked by engines and coaches purchased from the Metropolitan Railway and here is *Holdsworth* en route from Neasden to Pateley Bridge, photographed at York.

Later the NVLR purchased a Kerr Stuart steam railcar from the Great Western Railway and this worked the passenger service for some years. It was named *Hill* and is seen here at the Nidd Valley station at Pateley Bridge.

Thirty years after the line had closed the remains of *Hill* were found in a scrapyard in Leeds, still with GWR notices and fittings.

The LNER also used steam railcars but these were mainly of the Sentinel type, with water-tube boilers and chain or gear drive and having two, six or twelve cylinders. One of these cars has found a resting place at Darlington as a cricket pavilion.

RAILCARS—STEAM

In their prime the Sentinel cars worked many of the branch lines in the North Eastern Area of the LNER, and also the suburban services around some of the cities. They were particularly active around Hull, where the flat nature of the land suited the light two-cylinder variety of car. Here is *Eclipse* near Hessle in 1936.

For the more hilly routes a twelve-cylinder car was introduced. These worked mainly between Middlesbrough and Scarborough, and Whitby and Malton. It was the practice to give each type of car a trial run from York to Whitby, via Malton and Pickering, returning via Scarborough and the photograph shows 220 *Defence* at Whitby on such a run in 1932. A six-cylinder car is in the background and a G5 0-4-4T on the right is shunting in the goods yard on the banks of the River Esk.

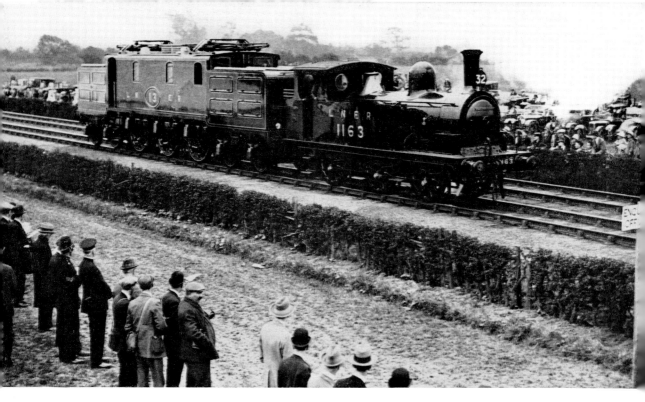

THE 1925 CENTENARY

A ceremony on a large scale was the procession of locomotives between Stockton and Darlington to celebrate the centenary of the Stockton & Darlington Railway. This was held on 2 July 1925 and fifty-three exhibits took part, most of them travelling under their own steam. However, this was impossible for the electric express passenger locomotive intended for the NER main line and it had to be towed by a shunting engine.

The procession was followed by an exhibition of rolling stock, models etc, at Faverdale wagon works. In addition, the locomotives from the procession were on display in the Works' Yard and here is a general view, with GN, NB and NE atlantics on the right and P1 2-8-2 2393 on the left.

THE HULL & BARNSLEY RAILWAY

The only railway to escape the clutches of the NER was the Hull & Barnsley, which ran between Hull and South Yorkshire; never, in fact, reaching Barnsley. It was built to connect the coal fields with the Humber port: passenger traffic never reached the hoped-for level and at the Hull end the passenger accommodation was provided by the insignificant Cannon Street station.

In readiness for the grouping of 1923, the HBR amalgamated with the North Eastern from 1 April 1922 and handed over a miscellaneous collection of 181 engines, many of which were soon withdrawn. The locomotive headquarters were at Springhead, on the outskirts of Hull, and the fine erecting shop was subsequently used to carry out repairs to engines stationed at HBR and NER sheds in the Hull area.

The HBR also worked the South Yorkshire Junction Railway between Wrangbrook Junction and Denaby. Stations were erected at Pickburn, and Sprotborough, but the passenger service was short lived and was withdrawn in 1903. Here is a Stirling domeless 0-6-0 at Pickburn.

The largest HBR mineral engines were the fifteen 0-8-0s built by the Yorkshire Engine Co. Here is one of them leaving Hull and passing Springhead shed: note the pit props on the first and fourth wagons.

In LNER days the coal traffic was handled by the ex ROD 2-8-0 of Great Central design. As the NER occupied the level route along the banks of the Humber the HBR had no alternative but to pass through the Wolds, necessitating heavy expenditure on tunnels and cuttings. Seen here is an 04 entering Sugar Loaf tunnel, between Little Weighton and South Cave.

The chalk Wolds produced hard water, and a water-softening plant was installed at Carlton Towers, seen here with one of the original Kirtley 2-4-0 engines as rebuilt with a Stirling domeless boiler.

Another Stirling feature was the horizontal pull-out regulator, shown in this cab view of 0-6-0 2520.

ANCILLARY SERVICES

The NER owned hotels in Hull, Newcastle, Saltburn, West Hartlepool and York and they were adver-tised as 'of great convenience and comfort, equipped throughout with the latest appointments, not to mention an excellent cuisine'. In every case they were the premier hotels in the town or city.

The view above shows the portico of York station in the left foreground, with the Royal Station Hotel beyond. Coloured postcards (bottom right) were issued to publicise the hotels.

Fire brigades were maintained by the NER at various centres and illustrated (bottom left) is a Merry-weather steam fire engine, complete with the NER coat of arms.

MODERATE TARIFF

REPLETE WITH EVERY MODERN CONVENIENCE

NORTH EASTERN RAILWAY HOTELS

ADJOIN THE STATIONS AT
YORK. HULL, NEWCASTLE-ON-TYNE,
SALTBURN. WEST HARTLEPOOL.

WAR AND PEACE

Damage to railway property occurred in both World Wars and the scene at South Shields (above) was photographed in 1941, when one of the South Tyneside electric cars had its back broken by a German bomb.

In Fletcher's time the North Eastern suffered a number of boiler explosions and that of 787 (below) took place at Blaydon in November 1878. Some parts of the boiler were found 283 yds away, whilst others were found on the opposite bank of the River Tyne.

MODERNISATION

Diesel traction was planned both by the NER and the LNER, and although experiments were carried out with various railcars and locomotives, it was left to British Railways to forge ahead with large scale diesel-isation. The first signs of the new order came in 1954 when multiple units were introduced between Harrogate-Leeds and Bradford. The use of these vehicles spread throughout the North Eastern Region and soon all except main line services were railcar worked. This view of a four-car set was taken on the historic Whitby & Pickering Railway.

The first main line locomotive to be seen in the Region worked the down Flying Scotsman from Kings Cross to Newcastle on 21 June 1958, returning on the 5.5 pm from Newcastle. D201 was the engine and it aroused the attention of the 'spotters' whilst standing at Darlington.

Since 1961 the Deltic diesel locomotives have set up a remarkable standard of speed on the east coast route, and on the famous forty-four miles between York and Darlington 100 mph is now commonplace. This stretch, opened by the Great North of England Railway in 1841, is now controlled by only six intermediate signal boxes, at Skelton Junction, Tollerton, Pilmoor, Thirsk, Northallerton and Eryholme. D9001, *St Paddy* passing the box at Tollerton, opened in January 1961.

For lighter goods duties, the 204hp diesel locomotive has become popular, and the illustration shows an engine of this type working the last train to Pickering on 1 July 1966.

THE REMAINS OF AN ERA

Now that steam locomotives have disappeared from British Railways' lines in the north east, the only examples of this fascinating breed will be in museums, or in the hands of preservation societies. Fortunately the NER Class H dock tank 1310 has been saved by a group of enthusiasts and it is currently in use on the Middleton Railway. Not only did this engine put in forty years' hard work on the NER and LNER but it was sold out of service in 1931 and then spent a further thirty-three years working for Pelaw Main Collieries and the National Coal Board.

And so we have come to the end of the steam era. Over the years countless men have devoted their lives to railways, all enriching history, if only by a minute amount. To salute them and to honour one of their most memorable colleagues I conclude with a view of the grave of George Hudson in the quiet churchyard at Scrayingham, in the East Riding of Yorkshire.

R I P

ACKNOWLEDGMENTS

Photographs for this volume have come from many sources and often it has been impossible to trace the original photographer. To these unknown my thanks are due for the many hours pleasure their work has given me. Many of them must have been dead for years considering that their photographs were taken a century or more ago. The colour illustration is reproduced by courtesy of Colonel Rixon Bucknell.

Without doubt the best ever NER train photographs were taken by the late R. J. Purves and two examples of his work are reproduced. In LNER days he was followed by two other photographers who are no longer with us, namely W. Rogerson and Cecil Ord. Members of the North Eastern Railway Association have kindly allowed me to use their photographs and from these I have chosen work by Ian S. Carr, Frank Dean, Douglas Hardy, K. E. Hartley, J. F. Mallon, T. E. Rounthwaite, S. E. Teasdale and Brian Webb.

Over the years I have been able to inspect the photographic files of various British Railways' departments, and in particular those built up at Darlington by the Chief Mechanical Engineer, and at York by the Public Relations Officer. To the various officers in charge of these files, and to many others in railway service who have given a lead to an elusive photograph, my grateful thanks.

J. Berry	7, 8
Ian S. Carr	9, 11 (top), 33 (centre), 64 (bottom), 67, 73, 94 (top)
British Rail (Eastern Region)	10 (top), 13 (top), 17 (top), 20 (top), 22, 23, 24, 25, 26 (top), 28, 29, 31 (top right), 31 (bottom), 34, 35 (top and bottom), 36 (bottom), 37, 38, 39, 41, 42, 43, 44 (top), 45 (bottom), 47 (bottom), 48, 49, 50, 51, 54, 55, 56 (top), 57 (centre and bottom), 58, 59, 60 (top), 61, 66, 68, 69, 70 (bottom), 74 (bottom), 75 (top), 77 (bottom), 78, 79, 81, 84, 86 (top), 87, 89, 90 (bottom), 92 (bottom), 93 (top), 99 (bottom), 100 (top), 101 (top), 103 (top), 104 (top), 105
Author	10 (bottom left), 11 (bottom), 26 (bottom left and right), 27, 31 (top left), 44 (bottom), 53 (top right and bottom), 62 (bottom), 65 (top), 71, 74 (top), 75 (bottom), 76, 80, 82, 83 (top and bottom left), 93 (bottom), 94 (bottom), 95 (top), 98 (bottom), 106 (bottom), 108 (bottom)
W. Rogerson	10 (bottom right), 45 (top)
Scarborough Museum	12 (top)
Author's Collection	12 (bottom), 13 (bottom), 14 (top), 15 (bottom), 16, 18, 19, 20 (bottom), 21, 30, 32, 33 (top), 35 (centre), 40, 46, 47 (top and centre), 56 (bottom), 83 (bottom right), 85, 88, 90 (top), 91 (top and bottom), 92 (top), 96 (centre), 97 (bottom), 99 (top), 100 (bottom), 101 (bottom), 102 (top and centre), 103 (bottom), 104 (centre and bottom)
R. J. Purves	14 (bottom), 15 (top)
C. Ord	17 (bottom), 65 (bottom), 70 (top), 106 (top), 107 (top)
W. L. Good	33 (bottom)
J. F. Mallon	36 (top), 52, 53 (top left), 60 (bottom)
D. Hardy	57 (top)
S. E. Teasdale	62 (top)
T. E. Rounthwaite	63, 64 (top), 91 (centre), 102 (bottom)
W. Huby	72
R. Parr Collection	77 (top)
K. E. Hartley	95 (centre and bottom), 96 (top and bottom)
Ian Lewis	86 (bottom)
S. L. Rankin	97 (top), 98 (top)
Brian Webb	98 (centre), 108 (top)
F. Dean	107 (bottom)

If the North Eastern Railway, its predecessors or its successors interest you, why not join the North Eastern Railway Association? The Association was formed to cater for enthusiasts and railway men interested in the railways of north eastern England and this book has been produced with the co-operation of members, who have placed their photographic collections at the disposal of the author. I am grateful to them for there help, and particularly to those members who have helped to locate obscure photographs.

Further details may be obtained from the Membership Secretary:

K. Hoole
Broughton House
Pickering Road
WEST AYTON
Scarborough
Yorks

INDEX